~~Maddie Brady~~

2019

Merry Christmas
Torren!

♡ Uncle Jason & Aunt JuJu

W9-BZR-214

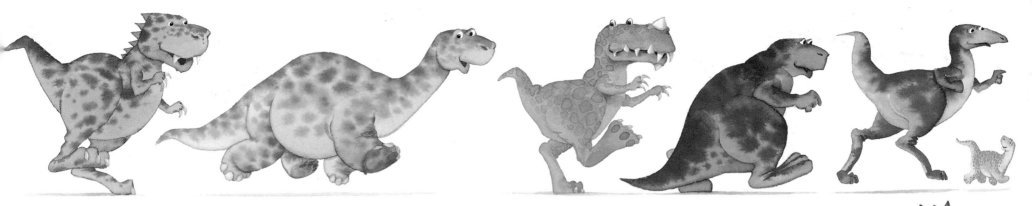

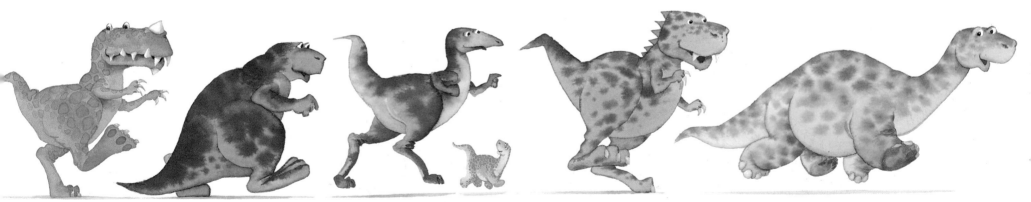

For John Smith

CD and paperback edition printed in 2006 by Ragged Bears
Publishing Ltd, Milborne Wick, Sherborne, Dorset, DT9 4PW

Distributed in the UK by Airlift Book Company, 8 the Arena,
Mollison Avenue, Enfield, Middlesex EN37NL.
Tel: 020 8804 0400

Illustrations © 1994 Paul Stickland
Text © 1994 Henrietta Stickland

First published in the United Kingdom in 1994.

A CIP record of this book is available from the British Library

ISBN 1 85714 367 1

Printed in China

DINOSAUR ROAR!

PAUL & HENRIETTA STICKLAND

RAGGED BEARS PUBLISHING LIMITED

Dinosaur roar,

dinosaur squeak,

dinosaur fierce,

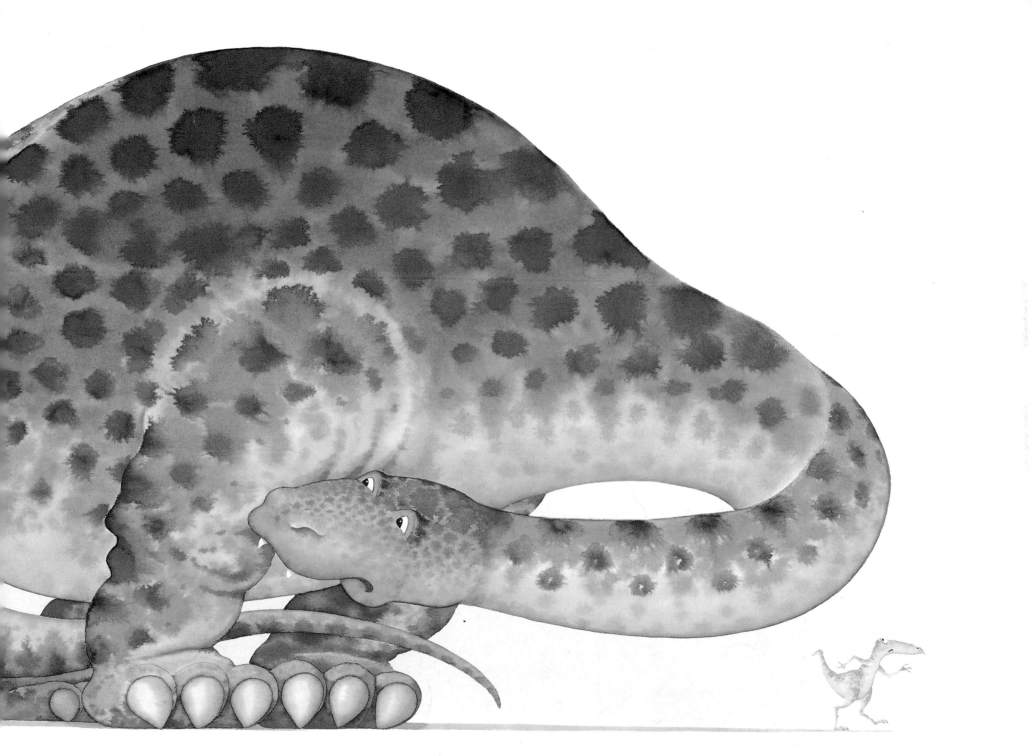

dinosaur meek,

dinosaur fast,

dinosaur slow,

dinosaur above

and dinosaur below.

Dinosaur weak,

dinosaur strong,

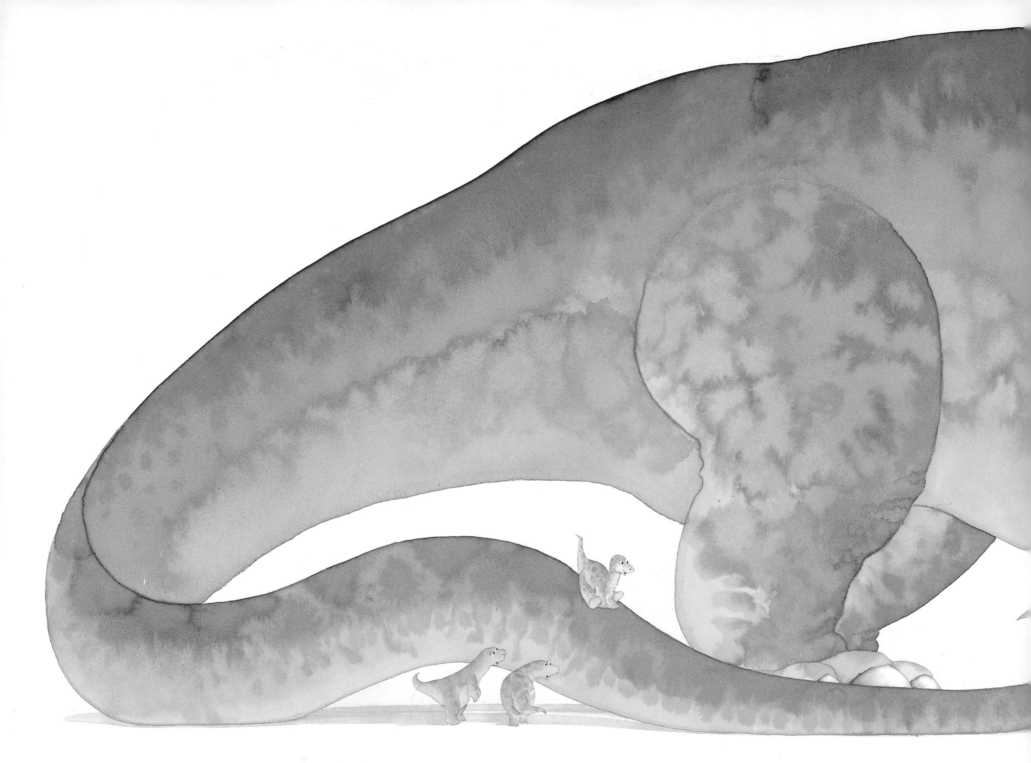

dinosaur short

or very, very long.

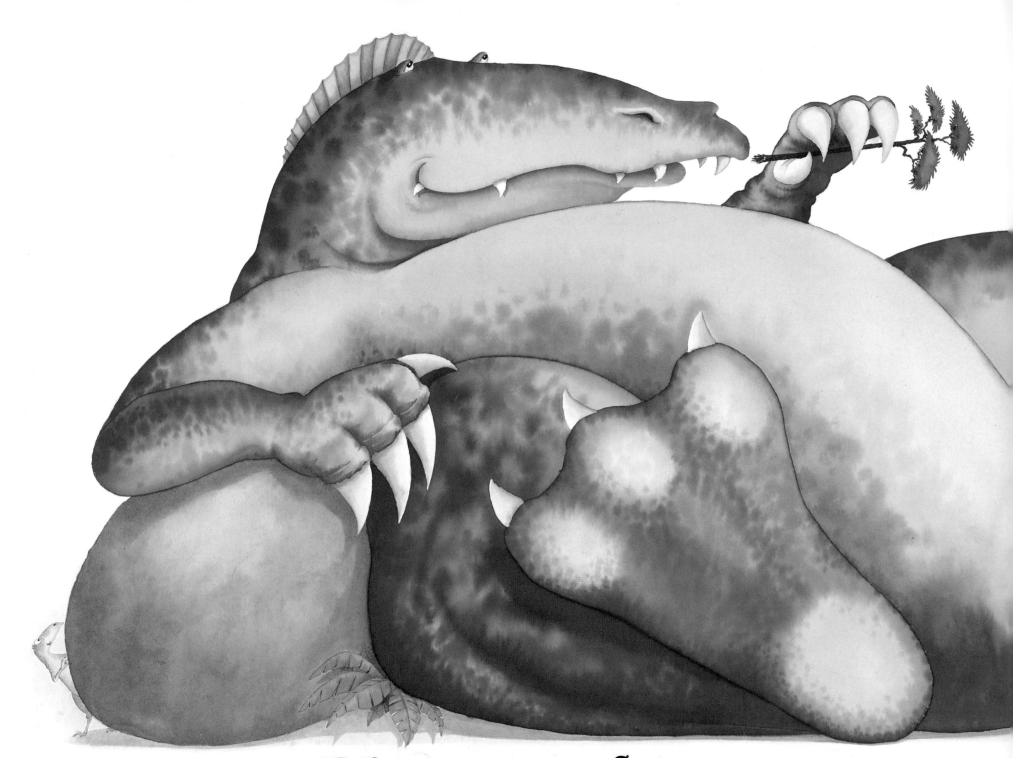

Dinosaur fat,

dinosaur tiny,

dinosaur clean

and dinosaur slimy.

Dinosaur sweet,

dinosaur grumpy,

dinosaur spiky

and dinosaur lumpy.

All sorts of dinosaurs

eating up their lunch,

gobble, gobble, nibble, nibble,

munch, munch, scrunch!